Praise for *Pittsburgh Will Steel Your Heart*

"Pittsburgh's unique character, beautiful landscapes and small-town charm always "steels the hearts" of visitors. For the people of Pittsburgh, Joanne's book shows how America's biggest small city has it all!"
—Mayor Luke Ravenstahl

I have often said that there is a "global" quality to music that helps bring people together. I am grateful that as conductor of the Pittsburgh Symphony Pops Orchestra I can be a part of that process. On the same note, I believe this book will bring the people of our city together in a meaningful way. Great job, Joanne, and thank you for including the Symphony as one of your reasons to love Pittsburgh!
—Marvin Hamlisch, Principal Pops Conductor

I am not surprised that the city as a whole, and its people and places, are so fabulous. There is a great innovative spirit here, both scientifically and culturally. Pittsburgh Will Steel Your Heart touches on many of the city's greatest achievements—every citizen should read it with a sense of pride.
—Dr. Tom Starzl, Distinguished Service Professor of Surgery at the University of Pittsburgh Medical Center

More Praise for *Pittsburgh Will Steel Your Heart*

Thanks to Joanne, the countdown to our region's 250th anniversary has truly begun. She's found 250 reasons to love Pittsburgh. Give a copy to your favorite Pittsburgher as an early "birthday present." And just imagine what you can do here!
—Bill Flanagan, Executive Vice President, Corporate Relations, Allegheny Conference on Community Development

As the head team physician for the Pitt Athletic Department, I have had a lot of interaction over the years with team members and their fans. It is always great to see how much people love their team and how often that love spills over to the city itself. Clearly Joanne is one of those fans who just can't get enough of Pittsburgh. Her book is a timely reminder of why we love our city so much.
—Dr. Freddie H. Fu, World-renowned Orthopaedic Surgeon at the University of Pittsburgh Medical Center

Cool ones! Blow your horn if you love this book! I expect to hear honking from every car on the Parkway. What a great way to celebrate the city's unique history, culture, and all that groovy food. Everyone in Pittsburgh should read Joanne Sujansky's fun, fantastic book!
—The Legend Porky Chedwick, Former Pittsburgh Radio D.J.

PITTSBURGH WILL STEEL YOUR HEART

250 Reasons to Love Pittsburgh

 Second Edition

A fun & fascinating look at what makes Pittsburgh unique . . . in honor of our 250th birthday in 2008.

Joanne G. Sujansky, Ph.D.
Certified Speaking Professional

ISBN-10: 0-9654465-7-3

ISBN-13: 978-0-9654465-7-0

Library of Congress Control Number: 2007938379

Published by:
KEYGroup®
1800 Sainte Claire Plaza
1121 Boyce Road
Pittsburgh, PA 15241-3918
800-456-5790
www.PittsburghWillSteelYourHeart.com
www.keygroupconsulting.com

Book Design and Production: Andra Keller, DeHart & Company Public Relations

Photos on pages 18, 22, 37, 45, 68, and 87 - Copyright, Pittsburgh Post-Gazette, 2006. All rights reserved. Reprinted with permission.

Photos on pages 13, 41, 47 and 73 by Kelly P. Hanna

Photo on page 15 by Sarah Anne Rosenkranz

Photo on page 35 by Mary Lou Ellena

Mr. Yuk emblem used with the permission of the Pittsburgh Poison Center.

Dear Pittsburgh Lover:

I can call you that, can't I? If you're not in love with our great city right now, you certainly will be by the time you read this book! Pittsburgh Will Steel Your Heart is a compilation of short, simple "word snapshots" of what makes Pittsburgh, well, Pittsburgh.

Twenty-eight years ago I founded KEYGroup, a consulting company that works with leaders to increase productivity and keep talent in their workplaces. This book came about as the result of several keynote speeches that I delivered about motivating and retaining talent in Pittsburgh. After giving the speeches, audience members began addressing me as an "Ambassador of Pittsburgh." Thus, I put this book together with the help of a diverse group of friends, business associates, and fellow citizens who share my sentiments about our fabulous city.

I LOVE PITTSBURGH! This city is where I live, work, and play and—hopefully—where I will eventually retire. There is a beauty, a vibrant spirit, and a unique culture in Pittsburgh that I have not found anywhere else on the globe.

Why did I write this book? Well, most obviously, I wanted to honor our city on its 250th birthday in 2008. But beyond that, I wanted to share the good news about Pittsburgh to the best of my ability—with businesses, with tourists, and with future and current residents.

This fun book, along with the equally "Pittsburgh-centric" web site www.PittsburghWillSteelYourHeart.com represents my very own grassroots campaign to tell the world about our great city. I hope you will join in.

First, share this book with friends. You can let them borrow your copy or, better still, you can buy a few extras to hand out. Second, please visit my web site often. Not only can you get more copies of this book there, you can order some other Pittsburgh items, and you can tell us what you love about Pittsburgh.

If you would like to get involved in my Pittsburgh promotion, I will be glad to help you brainstorm ways that you, your company, or your civic organization can join in the excitement. You may already have some ideas of your own . . . and I would love to hear them. I am excited about helping Pittsburgh "steel" as many hearts as possible. Join me, won't you? An entire city will thank you for your efforts.

Joanne G. Sujansky, Ph.D., Certified Speaking Professional
Founder & CEO, KEYGroup®
Pittsburgh, Pennsylvania

1

Once we were the world leader in steel production. Today we're well on our way to being the world leader in medicine, high-tech, and education.

2

Beautiful churches, big and small, featuring stained glass and steeples of all types, grace almost every neighborhood.

3

David McCullough, a two-time winner of the Pulitzer
Prize, graduated from Shady Side Academy.
Best known for his books, which include
The Johnstown Flood and *Truman*, he has been referred
to as "a master of the art of narrative history."

4

The Enrico Biscotti Company in the
Strip District makes the best biscotti
you will ever taste.

5

The Carnegie Science Center is known around the world
for exhibits and planetarium shows that travel across the
country and throughout Europe and Australia.
In 2003 the Science Center received the
National Award for Museum Service.

6

Pittsburgh has a long, rich history.
From colonial times through the present, and
from the French and Indian War through the
Civil War, Pittsburgh has been a focal point
for U.S. history. Spend an afternoon browsing
through the Senator John Heinz History Center
to gain a sense of the historic tapestry
that is Pittsburgh.

7

The hottest spot in town is the Pittsburgh Glass Center
at Penn and Friendship avenues, where ovens
for making glass can reach almost 2,400 degrees.

8

Isaly's chipped chopped ham, a unique way of shaving baked ham, is a refrigerator staple in most households even today, a holdover from the era when Isaly's dairy stores dotted the landscape of Western Pennsylvania.

9

People still ask where you went to high school.

10

Google opened an office here because it could
not get talented people to move to its
offices in California.

11

Most people know the Strip District for its ethnic grocery
stores and delicious produce—and yet few realize it has also
been home to a saint. St. John Neumann served as pastor of
St. Philomena, Strip District, from 1844 to 1847
and was canonized a saint in 1977.

12

In 2006, *Esquire* magazine rated Pittsburgh as
best among "Cities that Rock" in
the United States.

13

We're the only place in the world to
offer a Ph.D. in Robotics
(Carnegie Mellon University).

14

Streets that run neither parallel nor
perpendicular. Pittsburgh's "Golden Triangle,"
an apex formed by the converging Allegheny and
Monongahela rivers, made it impossible for city
engineers to lay out streets in the grid familiar to
most other cities.

15

We've used and revised the land. In fact, we rank
second in green-certified space among cities in the
nation and we are home to the world's
largest "green" building, the
David L. Lawrence Convention Center.

16

Lots of "mom-and-pop" pizza parlors making
delectable pizza with a wide array of toppings.
Where else but Pittsburgh are you going to find
a pierogi-topped pizza?

17

Football fans across America
acknowledge the fearsome reputation of
four Steelers named Green, Greenwood,
White and Holmes, known for eternity
as "The Steel Curtain."

18

Thanks to the clear water of the Allegheny River,
you can actually catch big fish downtown.

19

The word "yunz"—a true Pittsburgh original.

20

Director George Romero attended Carnegie Mellon University and is most well known for the movie *Night of the Living Dead*, filmed here in Pittsburgh.

21

George Washington slept here, several times. Between 1753 and 1755, Washington traveled to Western Pennsylvania three times on behalf of the Governor of Virginia.

22

America's first and most dramatic
"urban renewal" in the '50s and '60s
transformed our downtown area.

23

Senator John Heinz History Center, Pennsylvania's
largest history museum. It also includes the Western
PA Sports Museum and a Special Collections gallery.

24

The horrible disease of polio was itself crippled
by the research of Dr. Jonas Salk at
the University of Pittsburgh.

25

In addition to the numerous colleges and universities throughout Pittsburgh, there are also 89 trade and technical schools in the region, opening additional post-secondary opportunities for local students.

26

We're home to the National Aviary—the only bird zoo in the nation.

27

Pirate shortstop Bill Mazeroski's ninth inning,
two-out homer to win the 1960 World Series
is regularly named as one of the most dramatic
moments in sports history.

28

The right-field wall at PNC Park is 21 feet high
in honor of legendary Pirates right fielder
Roberto Clemente, who wore number 21.

29

The United States' first commercially successful plate glass maker
was the Pittsburgh Plate Glass Company (PPG), founded in
Creighton in 1883. It has paid its shareholders
uninterrupted dividends since 1899.

30

We have hundreds of miles of walking, hiking,
and bike trails along waterfronts and
through wooded hillsides.

13

31

Pittsburgh is a major, worldwide player in advanced computing technology, primarily due to Carnegie Mellon University, its Computer Emergency Response Team, and the Pittsburgh Supercomputing Center.

32

You can still go to drive-in theaters. The Dependable Drive-In located in Moon Township shows first-run movies seven nights a week and features an old-fashioned snack bar with burgers, fries, popcorn, candy and soda.

33

Spring in Pittsburgh is a spectacular explosion of greenery and blossoms that is especially vibrant after a cold winter.

34

Musical legend Perry Como was born
in Canonsburg in 1912.

35

The Pittsburgh region is home to 446 bridges,
the most of any city in the world.

36

The central rotunda, capped by a stained-glass dome, in the landmark Union Trust Building (now called Mellon One) is one of the most spectacular indoor views in the city.

37

There's nowhere else on earth where you can "redd up." In fact when the late Mayor Bob O'Connor assembled a team to clean up the city he relied on "Pittsburghese" to name it (what else) the "Redd Up Crew!"

38

Two-hundred-fifty-thousand people showed up for the Super Bowl XL Victory Parade held February 7, 2006. That's right . . . a quarter of a million people!

39

It's just a few miles to Moon and Mars.

40

One way to tell if someone's from Pittsburgh is to ask for a "loop of thin rubber that holds objects together" (as the dictionary defines it). You'll know they're from Pittsburgh if they give you a "gum band."

41

The Immaculate Reception.

42

The Pittsburgh region has been a spawn of movie talent, including Dick Powell, Michael Keaton, Jeff Goldblum, Jimmy Stewart, and Sharon Stone.

43

Pittsburghers are really caffeinated! We purchase more coffee—3.4 pounds per capita—than any other major American city.

44

Dinosaur Hall at the Carnegie Museum of Natural History has always been a cool place to hang out. But the new "Dinosaurs in Their Time" exhibit now provides one of the most exciting and interesting dinosaur exhibits ever!

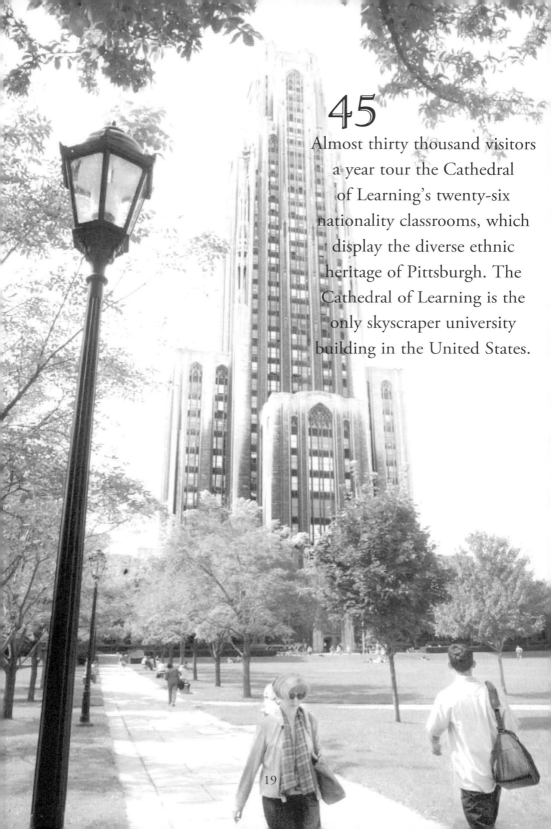

45

Almost thirty thousand visitors
a year tour the Cathedral
of Learning's twenty-six
nationality classrooms, which
display the diverse ethnic
heritage of Pittsburgh. The
Cathedral of Learning is the
only skyscraper university
building in the United States.

46

Gertrude Stein, American expatriate, writer, and confidant of Ernest Hemingway, was born in Pittsburgh in 1874. When speaking about her hometown once, someone asked her, "What's it like there?" She famously replied, "There is no there, there." Fortunately she was speaking about Oakland, California, where she later grew up.

47

The area is abundant in golf courses.
We rank first (or nearly first)
in number of places to play per person.

48

We have two degrees of separation instead of six.
Everybody in Pittsburgh seems to be connected
to everybody else.

49

Our broadcast celebrities are easy to talk
with and relate to.

50

Hanging over the railing of the Schenley Park Bridge
provides a terrific view of the man-made Panther Hollow
Lake. The marble panthers that grace the four corners of
the bridge were created by Giuseppe Moretti,
the famous Italian sculptor.

51

As if the accomplishments of Mario Lemieux
weren't sufficient for local hockey fans, the
Penguins 2005 draft choice, Sydney Crosby,
may have brought Pens fans a player who could
actually surpass the deeds of "Le Magnifique."

52

The downtown skyline at night
is spectacular—especially during
Monday Night Football.

53

In its annual "World in 2006" issue, The Economist
magazine rated 127 cities from around the world as best
places for business travel. Pittsburgh ranked #11.

54

On June 6, 1949, a small thirteen-seat drive-in restaurant called Eat 'n Park opened in Pittsburgh's South Hills. Ten carhops served the throng of customers that flowed along Saw Mill Run Boulevard. The restaurant had to close down after six hours because so many cars tried to pull into the parking lot that a huge traffic jam ensued. Needless to say, Eat 'n Park was able to regroup and re-open . . . and now it's famous for the happy face sugar cookie, "Smiley."

55

You can dance to polka music, the Electric Slide, and the Chicken Song at weddings.

56

There's no better view than sunset over the golden triangle when the golden bridges glow.

57

In 1886, The Pittsburgh Brewing Company—makers of Iron City Beer—became so successful that it had to move its operation from its original facilities on 17th Street to a four-story brick building on Liberty and 34th Street. The company's headquarters remain there today.

58

The Three Rivers Arts Festival, an awesome consortium of world-renowned artists, attracts thousands despite the rain showers in June.

59

We have five professional sports teams: the Steelers, Pirates, Penguins, Riverhounds and Xplosion.

60

The Christmas tree and skating rink at PPG Place.

61

Martha Graham, a pioneer in modern dance,
was born in Pittsburgh in 1894.

62

People may leave but they come back.
Despite promotions, transfers, new
jobs, schooling or other adventures ...
Pittsburghers always return home.

63

The Thunderbolt rollercoaster at Kennywood
Park remains at the top of everyone's "top
coasters" list by the National Amusement Park
Historical Association.

64

Our wonderful ethnic neighborhoods ...
Italian Morningside, German Troy Hill and, of
course, Polish Hill, to name a few.

65

Pittsburgh is where Elizabeth Jane Cochrane, a.k.a.
"Nellie Bly," started her journalism career in 1885.
She was hired by the editor of *The Pittsburgh Dispatch*
after writing a letter of protest about a
sexist article that appeared in the paper.
(Cool side note: She got her pseudonym from
a song by Pittsburgh native Stephen Foster.)

66

We have always had world-renowned maestros.
The Pittsburgh Symphony has been home to
Victor Herbert, Otto Klemperer, Fritz Reiner,
William Steinberg, Andre Previn, Lorin Maazel,
Mariss Jansons and Marvin Hamlisch.

67

The visionaries who have made their homes here-
from Dr. Jonas Salk, who cured Polio, to Dr.
Thomas Starzl, who pioneered liver transplantation.

68

Benefactors such as Scaife, Mellon, and Frick,
once renowned captains of industry, are now
household names for the foundations, museums
and art centers they funded.

69

From the Pittsburgh Symphony to the
Pittsburgh Ballet, the cultural district
is alive at night.

70

Christina Aguilera, a famous pop singer,
graduated from North Allegheny High School.

71

The Pittsburgh accent-nothing like it anywhere
else n'at. Here people say "dahntahn" for
downtown, "stillers" for Steelers, "Sliberty"
for East Liberty, and "Yunz" for "you all" or
everyone. In fact, if you talk like this you are
officially a "Yunzer."

72

Doo Wop groups like Johnny Angel and the Halos and Jimmy Beaumont and the Skyliners continue to entertain local "bobby soxers."

73

Shirley Jones, the mom on *The Partridge Family*, was born in Charleroi in 1934. After graduating high school, she entered the Miss Pittsburgh Pageant and won. She still visits our city yearly for family reunions.

74

Listening to accordion music while you wait for your fish at Wholey's.

75

In Pittsburgh so many things are within walking distance. You can walk the downtown area without doing a marathon—and without getting mugged.

76

Pittsburgh is the eighteenth most educated city in the U.S., with 33.6 percent of the population having a college degree or higher. There are forty-four colleges and universities in the Pittsburgh area.

77

We're the home of Sarris Candies, maker of the "World's Best Chocolate." The factory and ice cream parlor of this family-owned business occupies a space the size of a football field.

78

The Andy Warhol (born Andrew Warhola in Pittsburgh) Museum, a one-of-a-kind gallery devoted to American pop culture.

79

There's a niche for everyone. Whatever pleases
your palate, Pittsburgh has that flavor.

80

The Steelers were called the Pirates for seven
seasons. Founder Art Rooney renamed his team
the Steelers in 1940.

81

The airport is very efficient and convenient
and has a T-Rex that stands 15 feet high
greeting you when you arrive.

82

Walking across the Roberto Clemente Bridge for a Pirates game. And fireworks at the end of the game.

83

Visitors from around the world are stunned when the magnificent view of our downtown jumps out at them as they emerge from the Fort Pitt Tunnel.

84

Mellon Financial Corporation, now known as The Bank of New York Mellon, was the first major bank in the U.S. to introduce computers into the banking business. Installed in the early 1950s, IBM model 650 weighed two-and-a-half tons, took up a large room, and offered about the same computing power as today's pocket calculators.

85

People look forward to, celebrate, and decorate for all holidays—even Groundhog Day.

86

All the unique stairways from street to street leading to homes perched on the various hills in the city.

87

Pittsburgh is a Mecca for oldies bands and concerts.
Local groups such as the Vogues and Johnny Angel
and the Halos continue to sell out local venues.

88

Mary Cassatt, one of the leading members of the
impressionist movement, was born in Pittsburgh in 1845.
She spent most of her life in Paris, where she befriended
Edgar Degas and shattered the conventions that held
women back from pursuing art careers.

89

People nationwide doing business with
your company simply because
"they grew up in Pittsburgh."

90

"Meet me under the clock"—the Kaufmann's clock, of course. (Now owned by Macy's.)

91

An announcement about a possible cure for arthritis was made in a medical lab by people wearing Steelers jerseys.

92

We actually have four distinct seasons. But
Pittsburgh pundits say those seasons are: "Fall,"
"Winter," "Still Winter," and "Under Construction."

93

People are glad to spend 10 minutes (or more)
to try to give directions to strangers
who stop them on a corner.

94

You can still order from a drive-in carhop, Jerry's
Curb Service, in Beaver County, a mere
30-minute drive from downtown Pittsburgh.

95

With all the wild turkeys, skunks, deer, raccoons, and other creatures, your backyard might as well be a petting zoo.

96

Pittsburgh is a popular lyric for hit songs. Among the artists that have named the 'Burgh in their music are Simon & Garfunkel, Chuck Berry, Talking Heads, Bob Dylan, Lou Reed, Gordon Lightfoot, Frank Zappa, Bruce Springsteen, and Alabama.

97

Station Square: the place to go for dining, entertainment, shopping, and celebrating after ball games. You can park at Station Square and ride one of the Gateway Clipper boats before and after the Steelers, Pirates, and Panthers games.

98

Our fantastic state-of-the-art medical care and our variety of world-renowned hospitals. The University of Pittsburgh Medical Center, for example, is internationally renowned for achievements in transplantation, cancer treatment, neurosurgery, psychiatry, rehabilitation, geriatrics, and women's health, among others.

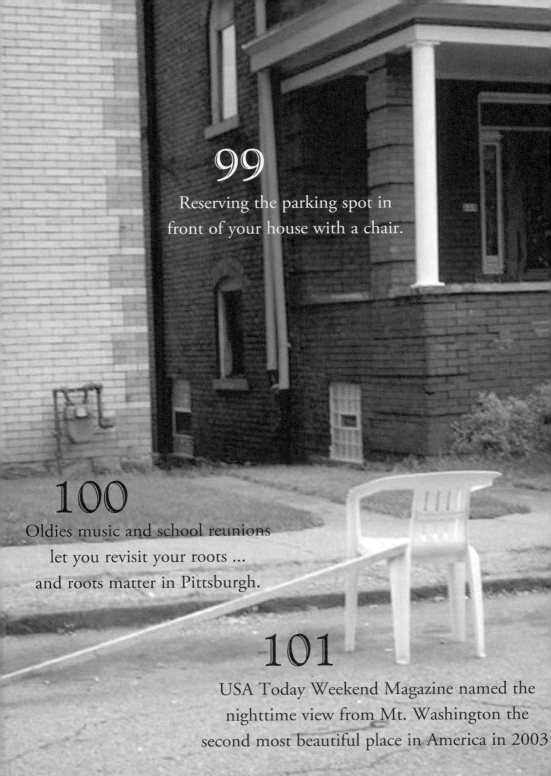

99
Reserving the parking spot in
front of your house with a chair.

100
Oldies music and school reunions
let you revisit your roots ...
and roots matter in Pittsburgh.

101
USA Today Weekend Magazine named the
nighttime view from Mt. Washington the
second most beautiful place in America in 2003

102

Two of the greatest baseball teams in the former Negro League, the Crawfords and the Homestead Grays, were sponsored here, producing greats like
Satchel Paige and Josh Gibson.

103

Tunnels are a way of life here. In fact, the Liberty Tunnel is the nation's first modern automobile tunnel. It was excavated before New York's Holland Tunnel and finished three years earlier.

104

All of our eccentric heroes: Former Mayor Sophie Masloff, Steeler Commentator Myron Cope, and "The Legend," Porky Chedwick.

105

Thermo Fisher Scientific, the world leader in serving science, has century-old roots in Pittsburgh. In 1954, Pitt researcher Dr. Jonas Salk used their reagents in the development of his polio vaccine. More recently, the company donated equipment for molecular and biotechnology labs at the Carnegie Museum of Natural History.

106

The Allegheny County Jail in Pittsburgh was the site of Mrs. Soffel's legendary crime—her home on the top of Mt. Washington is now a fine eatery.

107

When Lawrence Welk's orchestra, the "Champagne Music Makers," performed on television each week it was against a backdrop of rising bubbles from a "bubble machine" that was invented (where else?) in Pittsburgh.

108

When U.S. Steel was founded in Pittsburgh in 1901, it was the largest business enterprise ever launched. It remains the largest integrated steel producer in the country today.

109

The Vogues from Turtle Creek scored top ten hits with "You're the One" and "Five O'Clock World" in the mid 1960s.

110

The riverboats, especially the Gateway Clipper Fleet.

111

The place where two rivers come together to
make a new river, the Ohio.
(No other city has a triangle like ours!)

112

Pittsburghers will typically give you the shirts off their backs
(provided they're not Steelers, Penguins, or Pirates shirts).

113

Pierogies are a food group.

114

Mama Lena's Pizza House in McKees Rocks
officially contended for the Guinness Book of World
Records in March 2007 by creating the world's largest
commercially sold pizza. Their 150-cut, 53 1/2 inch pizza
sells for $99.99.

115

One of the more fun ways to see Pittsburgh is aboard
The Just Ducky tour boats, vehicles that travel the
streets for the first part of the tour then plunge into the
river to motor to the North Shore or the South Shore.

116

Pittsburgh: where the slightest hint of snow
sends people running to the grocery store
to stock up on bread and milk.

117

Founded in Pittsburgh in 1888, the Aluminum
Company of America (Alcoa) is the world's leading
producer of aluminum and was named one of the
top three most sustainable corporations in the world
at the World Economic Forum.

118

Jeff Goldblum, whose catchphrase "Must go faster!"
has been used in at least 11 of his films,
is a Pittsburgh native.

119

We have lots of people who volunteer.
Pittsburgh Cares, for just one example, maintains
a network of more than 3,500 people who
volunteer their time at over 100 nonprofits.

120

Shanice, a Grammy-nominated American R&B singer,
is a native of Pittsburgh. Interesting factoid: at the
age of nine, she starred in a Kentucky Fried Chicken
commercial with Ella Fitzgerald.

121

Real estate is reasonable. Pittsburgh is consistently ranked
as one of the best real estate markets in the country for
price and value, one of the reasons that the city scores
high in rankings such as the *Places Rated Almanac*.

122

The Steelers in the red zone at Heinz Field.
It's even more fun because we're the home of
Heinz ketchup.

123

Pittsburgh has many activities and programs for the
elderly, including numerous AARP chapters, senior
centers, bus trips, classes and cultural attractions.
Pittsburgh is a great place to "un-retire."

124

The Big Mac® was invented at a McDonald's franchise in
Uniontown in 1967.

125

Rachel Carson, the internationally renowned writer, was
born in Springdale in 1907. In honor of the naturalist,
Pittsburgh's Ninth Street Bridge was renamed
the Rachel Carson Bridge in 2006, as a result of the
efforts of Chatham University.

126
We are privileged to enjoy fabulous parks that allow us time to get away, commune with nature and recharge. Right downtown there's Point State Park, Schenley Park, Frick Park and many others.

127
Seeing the kayakers and rowing teams on all of our rivers. And we are home to Three Rivers Rowing Association.

128

The *Pierogies Race* at PNC Park. No matter how many times you see it, it is still funny.

129

You can view webcams of Peregrine Falcons that live downtown and at the Cathedral of Learning by visiting the Eastern Pennsylvania Conservancy website www.paconserve.org.

130

The green of the trees on the hillsides along the rivers in the spring. The red and gold of those same trees in the fall.

131

Barbara Feldon of *Get Smart* fame is a graduate
of Bethel Park High School.

132

The Pitt News, a financially independent
newspaper written and managed by students
at the University of Pittsburgh, soon will be
celebrating its 100th year of publication.

133

You <u>can</u> get there from here! Pittsburgh is located
halfway between New York City and Chicago and
is within a two hour flight or a day's drive of more
than 70 percent of the U.S. population.

134

The International Poetry Forum was founded in 1966 by
Duquesne University's Dr. Samuel Hazo and attracts
an international gathering of poets, writers,
and artists to the city every year.

135

Dennis Miller, the comedian and television/
radio host, is a product of the Pittsburgh Public
Schools.

136

When you have a block party, you actually
know your neighbors.

137

You can still find a high school student happy to cut your lawn. And kids still want to baby-sit.

138

You can't get a table anywhere on a Friday night without a 45-minute wait. (Why is this a positive? It proves we have great restaurants and a booming economy!)

139

Italian is the predominant ethnic food of choice.

140
School closings are major news events in January and February.

141
North Hills, South Hills, Penn Hills, Polish Hill, Squirrel Hill, and the Hill District—get the picture?

142

The most famous baseball card in history, the Honus Wagner T206, was sold in 2007 for $2.35 million, the most money ever paid for a baseball card. The card was printed to honor the legendary Pittsburgh Pirate shortstop, considered one of the greatest men to ever play the game!

143

There is nothing like a high school football game in October...priceless.

144

In 1987, the founder of 84 Lumber Company, Joseph A. Hardy III, purchased Nemacolin Woodlands Resort at an auction. He has turned it into a world-class resort that has one of the most distinguished art collections in the area.

145
Being so close to a top ski resort: Seven Springs.

146
Forcing the kids to go on a tour of Frank Lloyd Wright's Fallingwater and Kentuck Knob and them ending up loving i

147

Wonderful hideaway neighborhoods like Chatham Village on Mt. Washington, a 73-year-old, ivy covered, cloister of English-style brick residences. Not only a neighborhood, a historic landmark as well!

148

Pittsburgh jumped to the nation's third-best mid-sized arts city in a readers' poll released in 2006 by AmericanStyle magazine.

149

Festivals celebrating the various nationalities of Pittsburghers...Italian, Irish, Serbian and Greek, to name a few.

150

Fantastic and fun public pools where your stuff is safe while you are in the water.

151

The large number of parents who volunteer to coach youth sports teams.

152

The world's first gas station was a Gulf Station, located at Baum Blvd. and St. Clair Street in Pittsburgh in 1913. Of course, the prices have gone up since then!

153
You get to build a snowman
at least once or twice a year.

154
Home to music legends Henry Mancini, George Benson,
Billy Eckstine, and Lena Horne.

155

Bob Hope proposed to his wife, Delores, in Pittsburgh's William Penn Hotel, a historic landmark. Gee…Bob Hope was born before it was built!

156

Outdoor ice skating rinks, such as the one that appears in PPG Plaza each winter.

157

The word "Bingo" was first heard in America in the 1920s in Pittsburgh. Invented by Hugh J. Ward, the game expanded from local carnivals to national settings when he obtained a copyright and published a set of rules in 1933.

158

The Pittsburgh Debs, a women's open softball team,
won the 1970 & 1971 USSA World Championship.
Susan Stead was the 1970 MVP and
Jeri Riedel was the 1971 MVP.

159

The largest nativity scene-a replica of the
one in Bethlehem-is erected in the plaza of
the US Steel Tower every December.

160

December brings the Christmas tree on the old Horne's building (currently occupied by Highmark, Inc.).

161

Legendary Negro League and Major League baseball star Satchel Paige played here for the Pittsburgh Crawfords. In fact, many of the superstars of the Negro League, such as Josh Gibson and "Cool" Papa Bell, played in Pittsburgh for the Crawfords or the Homestead Grays.

162

We've been the temporary home to at least three saints: John Neumann, Francis Seelos, and Katharine Drexel.

163

Mr. Yuk, a green "yucky" face label warning children not to ingest poisonous substances, was conceived in 1971 at the Poison Center at the Children's Hospital of Pittsburgh. Mr. Yuk replaced the traditional skull-and-crossbones label, which research proved does little to deter children because they equate the Jolly Roger with pirates and excitement.

164

Our airport has the best shopping of any airport in the country.

165

Charlie Daniels hails Pittsburgh Steelers fans in
the song *In America.*

166

America's first radio station, KDKA, was started here in
1920 by the Westinghouse Electric Company.

167

Robert Morris University is named after a man
who helped finance the Revolutionary War and
who was one of three individuals who signed The
Declaration of Independence,
The Bill of Rights, and The Constitution.

168

We enjoy a rich history. Fort Pitt was a central location of what many believe to be the first true world-wide war, which we call the "French and Indian War."

169

Julie Benz, who played Darla in the television series *Angel*, was born in Pittsburgh in 1972.

170

The Duquesne and Monongahela Inclines are the remaining two of four inclines that carried passengers and freight up to the heights of Mount Washington, overlooking the city. Between 1870 and the turn of the century, 17 inclines were built throughout Pittsburgh.

171

No matter where you go in Pittsburgh, you're likely to run into someone you know.

172

The sight of towboats and barges cruising along the Allegheny, Monongahela and Ohio rivers has enthralled Pittsburghers since the 19th century.

173

Gardening is not a lost art.

174

Everyone remembers 1979 as the year the Pirates won the World Series and the Steelers won the Super Bowl.

175

Pittsburgh drivers are ultra-polite and will insist that you go first!

176

Pittsburgh is a great place to network and do business. Visit www.PittsburghWillSteelYourHeart.com to get started.

177

The Smithfield Street Bridge, built in 1883, is a historic landmark. It was the third bridge to be erected on the site, starting with a covered wooden bridge built in 1818.

178

Each Christmas Day over 300 volunteers from the Pittsburgh Jewish community brighten someone else's day as a part of the United Jewish Federation's day of volunteering: Mitzvah Day. Volunteers visit over twenty-five sites including hospitals, animal shelters and soup kitchens. To get involved in this community-wide event or for other Jewish young adult programming visit www.ShalomPittsburgh.org.

179

Iron City Beer drinkers were the first in the nation to enjoy the brewery's new "pull-tab" cans in 1962. It took a while to catch on, but eventually pull tabs spread to all beer cans throughout the country.

180

Schools are closed the Monday after Thanksgiving for the first day of deer (hunting) season.

181

Mystery writer Mary Roberts Rinehart was born here. She wrote 52 murder mysteries and coined the phrase, "The butler did it!"

182

Eating a hot dog at PNC Park on opening day is a perfect way to celebrate another new season of Pirate baseball.

183

The average commute to work in Pittsburgh is less than the national average.

184

Pittsburghers are strangely preoccupied with the weather, which gives us plenty to talk about.

185

For a fun Saturday, take the trolley downtown. Pittsburgh's "T" light rail vehicle runs from deep in the South Hills into the Golden triangle, where it becomes a subway with four stops beneath the city.

186

It's a great place to raise a family. In 2007, Worldwide ERC and Primacy Relocation ranked Pittsburgh as the sixth best city for relocating families.

187

The fact that the home plate from
Forbes Field is in Forbes Quadrangle at the
University of Pittsburgh.

188

The drive overlooking the Monongahela River on the
Boulevard of the Allies provides an impressive
view of steel mills, the South Side,
river traffic and numerous quaint neighborhoods.

189

How Pittsburgh has reinvented
itself over and over.

190

The mystery of the Mitchell B-25 bomber that crashed into the Monongahela River in 1956 and was never recovered continues to stir controversy. Theories continue to crop up regarding what the bomber may have been carrying and whether the Air Force secretly removed the bomber from the river bottom under the cloak of night.

191

People use the word "nebby" to mean "nosey." According to Carnegie Mellon University the term comes from the English term "neb" which refers to the nose or snout of an animal.

192

It's the only city where 6th Street and 6th Avenue run parallel to each other.

193

There is nothing like sinking your teeth into a Primanti Brothers sandwich.

194

When someone makes a list of the "most livable cities in America," we're *always* near the top.

195
Popular sports-only
talk radio shows.

196
Young people respect (and talk to) older people here.

197

Pittsburgh has more restaurants and eateries per capita than any large city in America.

198

The region has been a pioneer in the nuclear industry since after World War II. The first commercial reactor was constructed in Shippensport, near Pittsburgh. When the *Nautilus*, America's first nuclear submarine, sailed under the North Pole on it's maiden voyage, it did so with a nuclear engine built in Pittsburgh.

199

The "Steeler Nation" thrives. As of 2006 there were 975 Steelers bars across the U.S.

200
Our historic architecture reaches all the
way back to the 18th century!

201

Pittsburgh is the second largest inland port in America.

202

The abundance of trees (the Squirrel Hill Tunnel looks like it comes out of a forest).

203

Everybody in Pittsburgh forgets how to drive in the snow during the first snowfall of the season.

204

Free concerts at Hartwood Acres, the Point,
and South Park every summer.

205

The stellar Phipps Conservatory offers visitors
a pleasant stroll through a charming Victorian-
styled glass botanical preserve, filled with lush
gardens and beautiful displays.

206

Pittsburghers and residents from throughout the
region throng downtown for events like
"Light Up Night" and "First Night."

207

Exotic planes and jets soar high in the sky over
Pittsburgh during the annual air shows at
Allegheny County Airport.

208

Pittsburgh is home to not one, but two fully restored,
historically rich, world-class concert halls,
Heinz Hall and the Benedum Center.

209

Point State Park's fountain sprays 6,000 gallons of water per minute.

210

Game 4 of the 1971 World Series, played at Three Rivers Stadium, was the first World Series night game ever played.

211

Pittsburgh is the "City that Rocks" (according to Esquire Magazine). Concert goers can enjoy a wide variety of music to suit all tastes in many different venues, including Mellon Arena, Post-Gazette Pavilion, Pepsi Cola Roadhouse, The Palumbo Center, Club Café and numerous other locations.

212

"Le Magnifique" and "Super Mario" are affectionately respectful nicknames for hockey icon Mario Lemieux, who played for the Pittsburgh Penguins for 17 seasons (from 1984 to 2006). He will forever be regarded as one of the greatest hockey players in the NHL.

213

Pittsburgh's Oakland section is abuzz with college kids from numerous universities, including Pitt, Duquesne, Chatham, CMU, Robert Morris, Point Park and Carlow.

214

Memories of smartly dressed women who used to wear their white gloves and hats to shop downtown.

215

Nightlife on the Southside and in the Strip.

216

Twists and turns on Mt. Washington that make
San Francisco look tame.

217

Pittsburghers love French Fries. We love them so much we
put them on salads, in sandwiches, and on the side with just
about anything, including breakfast.

218

The rotunda and stairway of the Grand Concourse,
originally the Pittsburgh & Lake Erie train station
built in 1898, in Station Square.

219

We're no longer the "Smoky City."

220

People give directions based on "what used to be there."

221

A unique point of view on Pittsburgh history was photographed by "One-Shot" Teenie Harris- an African American who captured the essence of the African-American community in Pittsburgh.

222

The world's first Ferris Wheel was created by
Pittsburgh bridge builder George W. Ferris in 1893.

223

Myron Cope's Terrible Towel proceeds have helped raise
almost $1.1 million for the Allegheny Valley School,
which provides care for more than 900 people with
mental retardation and physical disabilities.

224

Libraries funded by Andrew Carnegie, who is said to have
given rise to modern philanthropy. After playwright August
Wilson—who grew up in the Hill District—dropped out of
high school, he continued his education on his own at the
Carnegie Library in Oakland.

225

The first movie theater in the United States,
named the "Nickelodeon" because admission was
a nickel, was opened in Pittsburgh in 1905.

226

We fought to retain the "h" at the end of Pittsburgh,
even after an edict from the U.S. Board of
Geographic Names ordered it to be removed.

228

Natives from mill towns may fondly remember the old days when plant workers walked home with their lunch buckets and thermoses.

227

The first Ice Capades performance was in Pittsburgh in 1940.

229

In 1979, decades before online shopping became a reality, Federated Investors, Inc., headquartered in Liberty Center, downtown Pittsburgh, invented EDGE (Electronic Data Gathering Extension), the mutual fund industry's first online order-entry system for purchasing and redeeming fund shares. Today, EDGEnet provides Internet account access.

230

There is no need to plant bulbs in the fall as the chipmunks eat them before they can bloom.

231

You can take a backyard composting class and receive a free compost bin from the City of Pittsburgh.

232

During the Civil War, Pittsburgh was one of the major suppliers of cannons and heavy guns to the Union cause. The cannons that manned the *USS Monitor* were made in Pittsburgh.

233

We have a lot of "mature" workers—
Pittsburghers don't like to retire.

234

Former Pittsburgh Steeler Jerome Bettis has gone from lighting up the scoreboard to lighting up television sports shows! But he still lives in the city and continues to invest in Pittsburgh businesses, including his new restaurant.

235

Pittsburgh is a regular fixture on "Top Ten Lists." Since 2006 Pittsburgh has been named:

- The sixth best for relocating families.
- The second-best city for home improvement professionals.
- The best arts destination in the country among mid-sized cities.
- One of the top 10 World's Cleanest Cities.
- The No. 1 place in America for baby boomers to find love and keep it.
- One of North America's top three "Cities of the Future."
- One of America's 50 hottest cities for business relocation and expansion.
- Seventh best city for Geeks.
- One of the nation's 25 Bargain Destinations.

236

The almond torte at Prantl's Bakery in Shadyside—
one bite and you'll crave it forever!

237

The Klondike Bar was invented by the Isaly family (of Isaly's chipped chopped ham fame).

238

We are close to Amish country.

239

Gene Kelly perfected his skills dancing between the raindrops in his native Pittsburgh.

240

Willa Cather, author of the classic American novel *My Antonia* worked for the *Pittsburgh Post-Gazette* early in her career and set one of her short stories in Pittsburgh.

241

America's most renowned bridge builder—John A. Roebling, who built the Brooklyn Bridge—perfected his engineering techniques in and around Pittsburgh in the 1840s to 1860s.

242

The Jeep was invented in Pittsburgh (by Willys
Mfg. Company in Butler in the late 1930s).

243

We're the only city where all the major sports teams have the same colors.

244

In 1940 the residents of Pittsburgh offered a $1 million reward for the capture of Adolph Hitler.

245

The first steamboat to ply western waters, the *New Orleans*, was built in Pittsburgh in 1811.

246

Pulitzer Prize-winning playwrights, August Wilson (1945)
George S. Kaufman (1889), and Marc Connelly (1890)
were all born in Pittsburgh.

247

At Candy-Rama, a favorite shop for young
and old alike, you'll find treats from your past,
including "old style" boxes that sold for 10 cents,
to conjure up fabulous memories.

248

The first community-financed television
station in the country was Pittsburgh's WQED.

249

America's landmark children's show, *Mister Rogers' Neighborhood*, was produced in Pittsburgh from 1967 to 2001.

250

It's home.

Now I would like to hear your reasons.

Why do you love Pittsburgh?

Visit www.PittsburghWillSteelYourHeart.com

and click on the "tell me what you love" tab.

Joanne G. Sujansky, Ph.D., CSP (Certified Speaking Professional)

For over twenty-five years Joanne G. Sujansky, Ph.D., CSP, has been helping leaders to increase business growth and profitability by creating and sustaining what she calls a Vibrant Entrepreneurial Organization. Her expertise, insight, wisdom, humor, and practical solutions have made Joanne a highly sought-after speaker for keynote addresses, seminars, conferences, and workshops. She has brought fresh concepts and effective techniques to executives and audiences in over thirty countries around the globe. Client favorites include the following topics:

- Keys to Creating the VEO
- The Vibrant Entrepreneurial Leader
- Culture: Your New Competitive Advantage

Among the organizations that have called upon Joanne to deliver speeches, develop custom presentations, and provide consulting services are: GlaxoSmithKline, International Federation of Training and Development Organizations, PPG Industries, Inc., U.S. Steel Corporation, PA Recreation & Park Society, Inc., American Express-Sweden, AT&T, Meeting Professionals International, U.S. Postal Service, IBM, Society for Automotive Engineers International, T. Rowe Price, Mayo Clinic, and Volkswagen, Audi, Porsche.

Joanne has authored numerous articles and books on leadership, change and retention, including:

- The Power of Partnering: Vision, Commitment, and Action
- The Keys to Putting Change in Your Pocket: Tips for Making Change Work for You
- The Keys to Conquering Change: 100 Tales of Success
- The Keys to Mastering Leadership: 101 Practical Tips
- The Keys to Motivating & Retaining Talent
- The Keys to Unlocking Your Potential
- Activities to Unlock Leadership Potential
- Pittsburgh Will Steel Your Heart:250 Reasons to Love Pittsburgh

Joanne, who founded KEYGroup®, is an award-winning entrepreneur. Earlier in her career, she held management- and director-level positions across several different industries. She is past national president of the American Society for Training and Development (ASTD), and is a recipient of their highest honor, the Gordon M. Bliss Award. An active member of the National Speakers Association (NSA), she has received their highest earned designation, Certified Speaking Professional (CSP).

Her energy and sense of purpose translate into winning presentations that audiences applaud. Packed with plenty of take-home value and on-the-job applicability, you can count on Joanne's presentations to provide your leaders with the keys to increase productivity and keep talent in their workplaces.

For more information, please visit www.keygroupconsulting.com, www.joannesujansky.com or www.PittsburghWillSteelYourHeart.com.

PITTSBURGH WILL STEEL YOUR HEART

Order Form

		Qty.	Total
Pittsburgh Will Steel Your Heart: 250 Reasons to Love Pittsburgh	$ 9.97		
Pittsburgh Will Steel Your Heart Long Sleeve T-Shirt – *Small*	$16.00		
Medium	$16.00		
Large	$16.00		
X-Large	$16.00		
XX-Large	$16.00		
Pittsburgh Will Steel Your Heart Button	$ 1.00		
Sujansky Says... Electronic Newsletter Subscription	**FREE**		
Sales tax (PA add 7%)			
Postage and handling will be added to orders according to weight.			
ORDER TOTAL:			

Ordering Instructions: Select the quantity of items you wish to order, record totals and send this form to:

KEYGroup®
1800 Sainte Claire Plaza ● 1121 Boyce Road
Pittsburgh, PA 15241
724-942-7900 (Bus) ● 724-942-4648 (Fax) ● 800-456-5790
email: sales@joannesujansky.com or www.keygroupconsulting.com

Quantity Discounts Available!
Call 724-942-7900 to inquire about Special Pricing
All items can be ordered at:
www.pittsburghwillsteelyourheart.com

** Complete Contact Information Required for Credit Card Orders**
** Information MUST match credit card **

Name: _____

Address: _____

_____

Phone: _____ Email: _____

Payment Options: Indicate your preferred payment method below.

❑ Check or Money Order   ❑ Credit Card: MC_____   VISA_____   AmEx_____
   (Make payable to KEYGroup)   Card Number:_____ Exp. Date:____/_____